SIMON AND SCHUSTER
BOOKS FOR YOUNG READERS
Simon & Schuster Building,
Rockefeller Center,
1230 Avenue of the Americas,
New York, New York 10020.

SIMON AND SCHUSTER BOOKS FOR YOUNG READERS
is a trademark of Simon & Schuster Inc.
Manufactured in the United States of America

10 9 8 7 6 5 4 3 2 1

Library of Congress Cataloging-in-Publication Data
Merriam, Eve . Mommies at work. Summary:
Examines many different jobs performed by working
mothers, including counting money in banks and building
bridges. 1. Mothers—Employment—Juvenile literature. 2.
Occupations—Juvenile literature. [1. Mothers—
Employment. 2. Occupations.] I. Eugenie, ill. II. Title.
HD6055.M47 1989   88-19796

ISBN 0-671-64386-X

Mommies at Work

by Eve Merriam • Illustrated by Eugenie Fernandes

Simon and Schuster Books for Young Readers
Published by Simon & Schuster Inc.
New York

Mommies make cookies to munch.

Mommies have laps to snuggle in.

 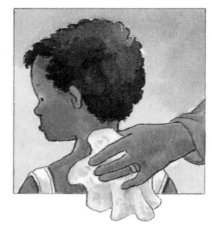 

Mommies wash dishes
and necks and ears.
Tie shoelaces and hair ribbons.
Find mittens that are missing.

 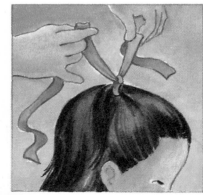 

Kiss places that hurt and places that don't.

Zip you in and button you up
and tuck in your favorite toys.

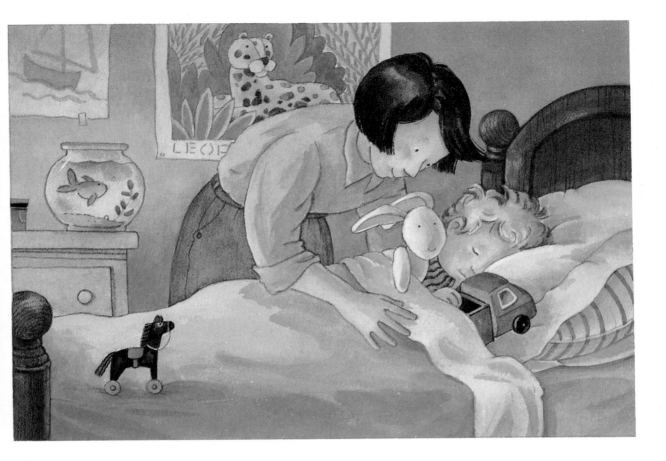

What other things do mommies do?

All kinds of mommies
do all kinds of work.
In tall office buildings,
in spread-out ranches,

supermarkets, stores—
all kinds of mommies
at all kinds of jobs.

There are dancer mommies.

Writer mommies.

Teachers.

Mommies
who are doctors.

Cashier mommies counting up money in banks.

Bridge-building mommies
with blueprints and T squares.

Television director mommies.

Mommies with telescopes.

Mommies punching tickets on trains.

Mommies in pet shops.

Mommies driving trucks.

Plugging in telephone wires.

Mommies at soda fountains pouring out chocolate ice cream floats.

Assembly line mommies building cars.

Circus mommies walking tightropes.

Sending signals in airport towers.

Factory mommies
stitching baseball gloves—

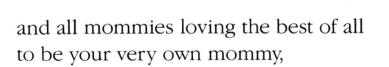

and all mommies loving the best of all
to be your very own mommy,